Songs For A Savior

Sermons And Worship Services
For
Advent And Christmas

David M. Oliver

CSS Publishing Company, Inc., Lima, Ohio

SONGS FOR A SAVIOR

Copyright 2003 by
CSS Publishing Company, Inc.
Lima, Ohio

The original purchaser may photocopy material in this publication for use as it was intended (i.e. worship material for worship use; educational material for classroom use; dramatic material for staging or production). No additional permission is required from the publisher for such copying by the original purchaser only. Inquiries should be addressed to: Permissions, CSS Publishing Company, Inc., P.O. Box 4503, Lima, Ohio 45802-4503.

Scripture quotations used in this book are from the New Revised Standard Version Bible (NRSV), copyright © 1989, by the Division of Christian Education of the National Council of Churches of Christ in the United States of America. Used by permission. All rights reserved.

Advent candle lighting ceremony adapted from "Blessings of the Advent Wreath" from the *Book of Blessings*, additional blessings for use in the United States of America © 1988 United States Conference of Catholic Bishops, Inc., Washington, D.C. Used with permission. All rights reserved. No portion of this text may be reproduced by any means without permission in writing from the copyright holder.

Excerpt from *In Search of a Father — The Tom Papania Story: From Mafia to Minister.* God's Saving Grace Ministries, P.O. Box 756, Powder Springs, Georgia 30127. Phone: (770) 590-8775, Fax: (770) 590-0130. Used with permission of Tom Papania. All rights reserved. No portion of this text may be reproduced by any means without permission in writing from the copyright holder.

For more information about CSS Publishing Company resources, visit our website at www.csspub.com or e-mail us at custserv@csspub.com or call (800) 241-4056.

ISBN 0-7880-1975-9   PRINTED IN U.S.A.

This book is dedicated to the wonderful people in United Methodist churches I have served: Asbury, Sandyville, Church of the Savior, Smithville, First U.M.C. Dover. Your patience, encouragement, partnership in ministry, and prayers have contributed immeasurably to my song for the Savior.

Acknowledgments

I am grateful to my colleague and friend, Dr. William Harvey, with whom I served for six years. Bill and I shared a deep devotion to Christ and an ability to celebrate and to utilize each other's gifts as we labored in ministry. The initial idea for this series was born during this fruitful season of service.

My wife, Jane Hoyt-Oliver, has been a wonderful companion and friend across 25 years of life and ministry. Without her incredible support, the journey of faith would have been much different. Jane, you have added immeasurably to my song for the Savior.

Michelle Oliver, daughter, friend, and devoted disciple, is filled with passion to pursue God and is being vigorously pursued by God. May you continue to hear clearly and follow the song which your Savior, Jesus Christ, has given you.

David M. Oliver
Epiphany, 2003

Table Of Contents

Preface 7

First Sunday Of Advent
Worship Service 9
Sermon: Zechariah's Song 13

Second Sunday Of Advent
Worship Service 21
Sermon: The Prophets' Song 25

Third Sunday Of Advent
Worship Service 33
Sermon: Mary's Song 37

Fourth Sunday Of Advent
Worship Service 43
Sermon: The Songs Of The Angels And Shepherds 47

Christmas Eve
Worship Service 55
Sermon: Our Song For The Savior 59

Preface

This Advent/Christmas worship resource and sermon series celebrates the deep song of faith which arises in response to a personal encounter with Jesus Christ, the Savior of the world. The design of the services and the messages invite people to draw near and hear again the Good News of faith.

The sermons are authentic, addressing the real struggles of faith as evidenced in biblical personalities such as Zechariah's wrestling to believe what the angel told him concerning the birth of his son, the prophets' search for God's word of hope in times of personal and social ferment, Mary's willingness to lay down her life for God's purpose, and the fear and joy intermingled with divine music as the birth of Jesus was heralded by angels and confirmed by the shepherds.

Ultimately, we are asked what our personal response will be to the Savior's birth. Will we allow room for a song of faith to rise in our day, in our families, churches, and community? The wonderful news is that the song is not so much what we create for God in response to Jesus' birth; it is a song that is birthed in response to meeting the Savior and receiving God's gift.

Grace and Peace,
David M. Oliver

Celebrating The Lord's Day
First Sunday Of Advent

Opening Sentence   Luke 1:68-69
    Blessed be the Lord God of Israel, for he has looked favorably on his people and redeemed them. He has raised up a mighty Savior for us in the house of his servant David.

Greetings
    We are blessed that you have chosen to worship with us today! May the living God draw near to you today and touch you at your point of deepest need.

Parish Announcements

Prelude Suggestions
Christmas Pastorale	G. Dinelli
We Would See Jesus; Lo! His Star	W. Reynolds

Choral Introit

*Call To Worship
Leader: As people long ago waited in anticipation of the day when the Messiah would come, we ask that our minds might be prepared so that Jesus is welcome.
People: **O come, O come, Emmanuel, come into our minds today.**
Leader: As people longed for the day when God would be more fully revealed through the Son, so we ask for pure hearts that Jesus might enter us.
People: **O come, O come, Emmanuel, come into our hearts today.**
Leader: As the people of God listened to the prophets foretell the coming of the Prince of Peace, and prepared their hearts and lives to receive him, so we pray for all barriers to Jesus be removed from us.

People: O come, O come, Emmanuel, come into our lives today.

*Processional Hymn   O Come, O Come, Emmanuel

*Welcome One Another
Please greet those around you and introduce yourself to two persons you do not know by name.

Advent Candle Lighting Ceremony[1]
Leader: Christ came to bring us salvation and has promised to come again. Let us pray that we may always be ready to welcome him.
People: **Come, Lord Jesus.**
Leader: We light this candle as a symbol of Christ, our mighty Savior. (*Light the first candle*)
All: **Lord God,
your Church joyfully awaits the coming of its Savior, who enlightens our hearts
and dispels the darkness of ignorance and sin.**

**Pour forth your blessings upon us
as we light the first candle of this wreath.
May its light reflect the splendor of Christ,
who is Lord, for ever and ever. Amen.**

Children's Message

Anthem Suggestion
Beautiful Savior   arr. Klein

Prayer Of Confession
Merciful God, we ask your forgiveness for preparing for your coming in mistaken ways; for spending more time with our holiday decorating than we do examining our spiritual selves; for thinking of our friends more as recipients of our gifts rather than persons with whom we can share your love;

for spending generously on gifts for our family while forgetting to give to those who are hungry and homeless; for being so busy with our shopping that we have no time left to worship and praise you for the true reason for celebrating Christmas. Forgive us, O God, in the name of the one you sent to save us, Jesus, our Emmanuel. Amen.

Morning Prayer And Lord's Prayer
Our Father, who art in heaven, hallowed be thy name. Thy kingdom come; thy will be done on earth as it is in heaven. Give us this day our daily bread. And forgive us our trespasses, as we forgive those who trespass against us. And lead us not into temptation, but deliver us from evil. For thine is the kingdom, and the power, and the glory, forever. Amen.

Giving Of Tithes And Offerings

Offertory Suggestion
A Celebration Of Carols — arr. B. Kroastad

*Presentation Response — Doxology
Praise God from whom all blessings flow; praise him all creatures here below; praise him above ye heavenly host; praise Father, Son and Holy Ghost. Amen.

*Prayer Of Dedication

Old Testament: Isaiah 43:18-19
Leader: God always blesses the reading of the Word.
People: Lord, open our hearts to you.

Special Music Suggestion
Infant Holy — arr. Rucker

*Gospel: Luke 1:68-79
Leader: This is the Gospel of our Lord.
People: Thanks be to God.

Sermon   Zechariah's Song
Part one in the series, *Songs For A Savior*

*Hymn   Hail To The Lord's Anointed

*Blessing

*Choral Response

*Postlude   O Come, O Come, Emmanuel
                                                        S. Caudill

* * * * *

*All who are able are invited to stand.

---

1. Advent candle lighting ceremony adapted from "Blessings of the Advent Wreath" from the *Book of Blessings*, additional blessings for use in the United States of America © 1988 United States Conference of Catholic Bishops, Inc., Washington, D.C. Used with permission. All rights reserved. No portion of this text may be reproduced by any means without permission in writing from the copyright holder.

Zechariah's Song
Part one in the series: Songs For A Savior
First Sunday Of Advent

Isaiah 43:18-19; Luke 1:68-79

Today begins the four-week period of preparation known as Advent. Advent comes from a Latin word, *adventus*, which means "to come" in the sense of a coming into place, coming into view, coming into being or arrival. We are to use this opportunity to prepare ourselves by looking back, remembering and celebrating the first coming of Christ, and by looking forward to Christ's second coming.

Advent is a time between two times. Christians acknowledge with gladness the wonderful, mysterious arrival of God in the world as a human being in the person and work of Jesus. We also anticipate with joy and hope the fulfillment of Jesus' promise to return to rule the earth as King of kings and Lord of lords.

Advent provides the occasion for us to reflect on what it means to live between these two significant realities. We are challenged to grapple with how to be faithful witnesses to the living God and his Son, Jesus, while we await with eagerness the consummation of all God's plans for Creation.

Zechariah's story, found in the Gospel of Luke, provides significant lessons on how to be faithful in the in-between times. Before getting to this, however, we must understand the background and context of this exciting story.

Zechariah was a Jewish priest near the end of King Herod's reign (5-4 B.C.). As a priest, Zechariah served at the Temple in Jerusalem for two one-week periods a year. He was a member of one of 24 divisions of priests or one of approximately 18,000 priests. A priest only officiated at the sacrifice once in his life, having been selected by the casting of lots. The setting for Zechariah's encounter with God was one of two times set aside daily for prayer in the Temple (9:00 a.m. or 3:00 p.m.). This took place as a part of the Israelites' perpetual offering to God as required in the Old Testament book of Exodus 29:38-42.

Zechariah was offering incense to God in the Temple as an act of worship and as an appeal to God for the forgiveness of the sins of his people. At that precise moment, God decided to act on behalf of Zechariah and on behalf of the people of Israel. God sent a messenger, the angel Gabriel, to speak to Zechariah. The appearance of the heavenly figure surprised and frightened Zechariah. But Gabriel said:

> *Do not be afraid, Zechariah, for your prayer has been heard. Your wife Elizabeth will bear you a son, and you will name him John. You will have joy and gladness, and many will rejoice at his birth, for he will be great in the sight of the Lord. He must never drink wine or strong drink; even before his birth he will be filled with the Holy Spirit. He will turn many of the people of Israel to the Lord their God. With the spirit and power of Elijah he will go before him, to turn the hearts of parents to their children, and the disobedient to the wisdom of the righteous, to make ready a people prepared for the Lord. Zechariah said to the angel, "How will I know that this is so? For I am an old man, and my wife is getting on in years." The angel replied, "I am Gabriel. I stand in the presence of God, and I have been sent to speak to you and to bring you this good news. But now, because you did not believe my words, which will be fulfilled in their time, you will become mute, unable to speak, until the day these things occur."*
>
> — Luke 1:13-20

Zechariah's unbelief resulted in him being both mute and deaf. He could only communicate with others through the use of a writing tablet (Luke 1:63). This time of silence contained a very important lesson for Zechariah. It meant that he was to listen to God and trust that God would do what God promised. Despite his age and the age of his wife, Elizabeth, God was prepared to act on their behalf. This birth also became a symbol and a sign of God's willingness to act on behalf of the nation of Israel, to give them both a Savior and one who would precede the Savior and prepare people's hearts for his coming.

I would like to lift up four faith lessons from this scripture. First, be *open*. God often acts on behalf of God's people in *surprising* ways. When we pray, as Zechariah and Elizabeth did, we must be open to how God intends to answer our prayers. God does not always act in ways that are predictable, understandable, or sensible to us at the time. In Isaiah 43:19 God declares, "Behold, I am doing a new thing; now it springs forth, do you not perceive it? I will make a way in the wilderness, rivers in the desert."

How many of us have experienced God's answers to prayers that were different from what we expected? This is not uncommon among people of prayer. *God does not always answer prayer as we desire.* When God answers prayer in unexpected ways, our job is to ponder God's answers and try to understand what God is seeking to communicate. Rather than being disappointed, surprised, or upset, we are better off asking God the question, "Lord, what are you trying to say to me through these circumstances?" We then need to take time to be silent and listen to God. Examine what God's Word says. Consult with mature Christians. Try to determine what God is saying to you through the ways in which your prayers have been answered.

The second lesson is to be *expectant*. When we pray, we can and should expect that God will act in some way. Zechariah's prayer for a son seemed to be halfhearted. He did not seem to be expecting such an answer. He had significant doubt rather than significant trust and faith. He raised questions with Gabriel. He looked at the obstacle of age rather than the sovereignty of God who hears and answers prayer. Don't we do the same thing? We look at what we consider the "realities" and draw our own conclusions as to what God is or is not capable of doing. God wants us to step into God's realities and experience God's perspective rather than limit God with our own thinking. God's kingdom thinking is open and expectant. This causes us to pray boldly and eagerly. We start to see things from God's unlimited vision rather than filtering everything through our limited perspective and our narrow experience of God. When this happens, we begin to see God work powerfully in both natural and supernatural ways. We discover that God's power is unlimited. This, in turn, encourages our faith, our prayer life, our trust in God, and our reliance on God.

Through John's birth, God revealed to Zechariah that he was renewing his redemptive, healing work among the people of God. A time of restoration and hope was promised. Not only was the social curse of barrenness lifted from Elizabeth, the spiritual barrenness of the entire nation was being lifted as well. Instead of impotence and a discouraging lack of faith, God was in the process of restoring repentance, new faith, and new life through the miraculous births of John the Baptist and Jesus the Christ. God's blessings were unfolding for individuals and for the entire community of faith. God was raising up a Savior and Zechariah's son, John, was to point the way to him.

Third, in addition to being open and expectant, we need to be *watchful*. God often leaves indicators of divine work, if we just keep our eyes and hearts open to them. Rarely does God just show up. God does not suddenly send a Savior to make us right with God and to offer us forgiveness. God calls people to be prepared to receive his coming. God wants us to embrace a new way of life, not as the basis of salvation, but in response to God's goodness and his salvation in Jesus.

When anyone makes a decision to follow Christ, he/she will usually be able to look back and see how God has used many people, events, and circumstances to draw him/her to the place where faith in Christ became possible.

I distinctly remember a man coming to church a few years ago and talking about his desperate need for God. A number of the staff ministered to him on several occasions. When he and I talked, he kept saying over and over, "I am lost. I need to find God. I *need* to find God!" I tried to listen to God as well as to the man's desperate words. I wanted to help him find God. He had prayed to receive Christ over and over but, seemingly, to no avail. He was still bound by his sinful behavior, his past, and his wasted life. Finally I said, "Brother, you wouldn't even be calling out to God and declaring your need for God unless God had already been searching for you! You may feel lost and alone, but God has been seeking you and drawing you or you would not even be here. You are valuable to

God! Don't give up hope! Look back over your life and ask God to help you see the times when he has been at work on your behalf. Be watchful for the work of God in this moment and listen to what God is trying to say to you today. Keep praying and, in God's time, you will receive what you are needing. Jesus said, 'No one can come to me unless the Father who sent me draws him; and I will raise him up at the last day' (John 6:44)." The encouragement seemed to make sense to this restless, confused man and give him some comfort. Following this, we prayed together. God continued the healing work in his broken heart and shattered life. God was powerfully present as the Holy Spirit continued to break down the barriers the man had erected. Praise God! The Lord can do this in your life as well. Be mindful of and watchful for the things God is doing in your life.

We have learned that we need to be open, expectant, and watchful. Fourth, we also need to be *teachable*. This lesson is drawn from Zechariah's and Elizabeth's experience. This reminds us that no matter what our age, we have more to learn from God. As we wait on God and listen to God, we are teachable. This becomes the doorway through which more grace is received, faith is renewed, our true, spiritual speech is regained, and our spiritual hearing is restored. We are never to grow spiritually complacent, prideful, or satisfied. If we are open and receptive, God always has much more to teach us.

Just about the time we think we know how God acts and what God is doing, God pulls us up short. God desires our dependence on him instead of depending on what we have learned about God. The Sovereign God wants each of us to remain open, malleable, adjustable. We are to be the Lord's instruments in the world, continually growing, continually sharing what we have learned with others.

The scripture indicates that Zechariah's and Elizabeth's hearts were righteous before God and they lived blamelessly (Luke 1:6). Nevertheless, they still had things to learn and needed God's help in the midst of the disappointments and discouragements of life. To their credit, despite their unusual circumstances and the deep disappointments they had experienced in life, they remained steadfast and faithful. During the nine months of enforced silence and a miraculous pregnancy, Zechariah and Elizabeth learned much about God's sovereign power, love, and willingness to act on behalf of his people.

This couple learned the value of listening to and trusting in God. God worked mightily in Zechariah and in Elizabeth so that when it came time to name the child on the eighth day of his life, both were obedient to the message given by Gabriel, "You will name him John" (Luke 1:13). They went against the cultural tradition of naming the first male child after his father. Instead, they gave him the name, John, meaning "Gift of God" or "God is gracious." At that moment of obedience, Zechariah was filled with the Holy Spirit. His mouth was opened and he was given speech again. He broke forth in a song of praise to God:

> *Blessed be the Lord God of Israel, for he has looked favorably on his people and redeemed them. He has raised up a mighty savior for us in the house of his servant David, as he spoke through the mouth of his holy prophets from of old, that we would be saved from our enemies and from the hand of all who hate us.*

He continued by blessing his child.

> *... And you, child, will be called the prophet of the Most High; for you will go before the Lord to prepare his ways, to give knowledge of salvation to his people by the forgiveness of their sins. By the tender mercy of God, the dawn from on high will break upon us, to give light to those who sit in darkness and in the shadow of death, to guide our feet into the way of peace.*
> — Luke 1:67-79

The lessons of silence, of listening to God, and of being obedient to God are as invaluable to us as they were to Zechariah and Elizabeth. Are we humble before God, allowing God to lead us and direct us, even if God's ways seem unconventional? Do we expect to conform to God's ways, purposes, and plans for us? Are we *open* to God's ways or do we insist that God must work in our way and according to our timetable?

When it comes to prayer, do we pray *expecting* God to act? Do we then *watch* to see how God is acting and lift up these answered prayers for the community of faith to see, hear, and rejoice? Are we *teachable*?

I would remind us that a pleasant outcome is not guaranteed to all who pray and are faithful. The Bible does not promise this. Zechariah and Elizabeth certainly faced many disappointments despite their faithfulness. What this passage of scripture underscores is that God is often at work in unexpected ways. Our job as persons of faith is to pray and try to discern what God is doing. As we listen to God and watch for what God is doing, then we can unite our prayers with the will of God. We can become partners in the Lord's loving, saving, re-creating activity in the world. May this Advent season be a time where you and I commit to joining God in God's exciting work in this church, community, and the wider world.

Let us pray. Almighty, sovereign, loving God, thank you for the refreshing lessons of faith to be drawn from the sweet-water well of your Word. Open our minds to make other connections and to allow you opportunity to build new bridges of understanding and faith. Help us to remain teachable, to desire to learn and grow even through the disappointments, trials, and struggles of life. Thank you for not giving up on us. Thank you for taking the initiative to act on our behalf in surprising ways. Praise you for always answering prayer as we need rather than as we desire. Open our eyes and hearts to see your glorious hand at work in our lives, our church, this community, and the world. Inspire and empower us to join you in that great work. We trust that as we do, you will take care of us and of all your people, according to your loving will and generous grace. We offer ourselves to you this Advent and pray for your guidance in our lives throughout this season and in the new year. In Jesus' name, we pray. Amen.

Celebrating The Lord's Day
Second Sunday Of Advent

Opening Sentence Micah 5:2
"But you, O Bethlehem of Ephrathah, who are one of the least of the little clans of Judah, from you shall come forth for me one who is to rule in Israel, whose origin is from of old, from ancient days."

Greetings
We are blessed that you have chosen to worship with us today! May the living God draw near you today and touch you at your point of deepest need.

Parish Announcements

Prelude Suggestions
Carol Medley   Hayes
While Shepherds Watched   M. Mauro-Cottone
I Wonder As I Wander   J. J. Niles

Choral Introit

*Call To Worship
Leader: O come, let us adore him, Christ the Lord! He will establish justice upon the earth. Distant lands eagerly wait for his teaching.
People: O come, let us adore him, Christ the Lord!
Leader: He will open the eyes of the blind and set free those who sit in dark prisons.
People: O come, let us adore him, Christ the Lord!

*Processional Hymn   O Come, All Ye Faithful

*Welcome One Another
Please greet those around you and introduce yourself to two persons you do not know by name.

Advent Candle Lighting Ceremony[1]
Leader: Christ came to bring us salvation and has promised to come again. Let us pray that we may always be ready to welcome him. (*Light the first candle*)
People: Come, Lord Jesus.
Leader: That the keeping of Advent may open our hearts to God's love. (*Light the second candle*)
People: Come, Lord Jesus.
Leader: Two Advent candles have been lit as a symbol of Christ, our present and coming Lord whom God has given to us.
All: Lord God,
your Church joyfully awaits the coming of its Savior,
who enlightens our hearts
and dispels the darkness of ignorance and sin.

Pour forth your blessings upon us
as we light the candles of this wreath.
May their light reflect the splendor of Christ,
who is Lord, for ever and ever. Amen.

Children's Message

Anthem Suggestions
Break Forth O Beauteous Heavenly Light   J. S. Bach
Will We Know Him?   Besig

Call To Confession   Isaiah 40:3-4
"A voice cries out, 'Prepare in the wilderness a road for the Lord! Clear the way in the desert for our God! Fill every valley; level every mountain. The hills will become a plain, and the rough country will be made smooth.'"

Prayer Of Confession
God, forgive us for we are fragmented persons. We are pulled in many directions. We pursue goals that are sometimes contradictory. We are concerned for the poor but not enough

to change our lifestyle. We feel sympathy for those weighed down by the burdens of life but we also resist getting involved. We see those who are victimized by their own sin and by abusive relationships yet we justify our distance by thinking there is nothing we can do to help. Forgive us, O God. Let this season be a time of healing for us. Through your compassion, have mercy upon us and help us to have mercy on others. Help us to cast aside our doubts and fears and to place our whole trust in your promise of life. Through Jesus Christ, the giver of life, we pray. Amen.

Words Of Assurance Isaiah 40:2

"Comfort my people," says our God. "Comfort them! Encourage the people. Tell them they have suffered long enough and their sins are now forgiven."

Silent Prayer

Pastoral Prayer And Lord's Prayer

Our Father, who art in heaven, hallowed be thy name. Thy kingdom come; thy will be done on earth as it is in heaven. Give us this day our daily bread. And forgive us our trespasses, as we forgive those who trespass against us. And lead us not into temptation, but deliver us from evil. For thine is the kingdom, and the power, and the glory forever. Amen.

Giving Of Tithes And Offerings

Offertory Suggestions

Mary's Boy Child	J. Hairston
Lullay, Thou Little Tiny Child	
with Infant Holy, Infant Lowly	Torrans

*Presentation Response Doxology

Praise God from whom all blessings flow; praise him all creatures here below; praise him above ye heavenly host; praise Father, Son and Holy Ghost. Amen.

*Prayer Of Dedication

First Lesson: Isaiah 11:1-9
Leader: God always blesses the reading of the Word.
People: Lord, open our hearts to you.

Second Lesson: Micah 5:2-4
Leader: This is the word of the Lord.
People: Thanks be to God.

Sermon   The Prophets' Song
Part two in the series, *Songs For A Savior*

*Hymn Suggestions
   I Want To Walk As A Child Of The Light
   Lo, How A Rose E'er Blooming

*Blessing
   If you wish, you are invited to join hands for the Blessing. Before you depart, greet those around you. Introduce yourself to people you don't know by name.

*Congregational Response   Let Us Now Depart In Thy Peace

*Postlude Suggestions
   Shepherds, Rejoice   D. Luca
   Festive March in D   Rebikoff

* * * * *

*All who are able are invited to stand.

---

1. Advent candle lighting ceremony adapted from "Blessings of the Advent Wreath" from the *Book of Blessings*, additional blessings for use in the United States of America © 1988 United States Conference of Catholic Bishops, Inc., Washington, D.C. Used with permission. All rights reserved. No portion of this text may be reproduced by any means without permission in writing from the copyright holder.

The Prophets' Song
Part two in the series: Songs For A Savior
Second Sunday Of Advent

Isaiah 11:1-9; Micah 5:2-4

I began last week's message by saying, "Advent is a time between two times." During the Advent season, we look back with thanksgiving on the first coming of Jesus Christ in humility and vulnerability as an infant. We look forward with hope to the second coming of Christ in power and glory. Advent provides the occasion for us to reflect on what it means to live between these two significant realities. We are challenged to grapple with what it means to be faithful witnesses to the living God and his Son, Jesus, while we await with eagerness the consummation of all God's plans for Creation. As we found in "Zechariah's Song," we can best do this by being open, expectant, watchful, and teachable.

Today we examine the "Prophets' Song" and explore what the prophets Isaiah and Micah have to say to us about living faithfully in this in-between time. Isaiah and Micah were contemporaries, although their audiences were quite different. Both were called by God in the latter part of the eighth century before Christ. Isaiah was born in Jerusalem and was related to the royal family. Micah came from Moresheth, near Gath, about thirty miles southwest of Jerusalem.

Isaiah was very much aware of and involved with the politics of Jerusalem. His heritage gave him an inside track on what was happening in national and international politics. He spoke to the sophisticated and the elite. Micah, by contrast, having been born and raised in a rural area, was less familiar with the inside matters of Jerusalem. He lived near the coastal road over which traders, pilgrims, and soldiers traveled between Egypt, Jerusalem, and points to the north. He addressed concerns about the moral and spiritual corruption brought by foreign alliances and their negative impact on both the Northern and Southern Kingdoms.

By that time in history, the nation had been divided. The Northern Kingdom was called Israel with Samaria as its capital. The Southern Kingdom was known as Judah with Jerusalem as its capital. During Isaiah's and Micah's prophetic term, the Northern Kingdom made an alliance with Syria and attacked the Southern Kingdom (ca. 740 B.C.). This alliance was unsuccessful and was later defeated by another strong enemy, the Assyrians, who destroyed Samaria and took over the Northern Kingdom (722 B.C.). The Assyrians also pushed forward to Jerusalem and laid siege to it. Had it not been for the intervention of God, the holy city would have been defeated as well.

In the midst of this vortex of international intrigue and spiritual turmoil, these prophets were commissioned by God to speak to the people. We will focus on the two passages we read this morning. Both texts are messianic in nature. In other words, they address the hope that God's Anointed One will be raised up and will bring help and renewal to a nation in the throes of seismic change.

In the midst of the siege by the Assyrians, Micah declared hope. This hope came in a strange form and from a strange place. "But you, O Bethlehem of Ephrathah, who are one of the little clans of Judah, from you shall come forth for me one who is to rule in Israel, whose origin is from old, from ancient days" (Micah 5:3).

Bethlehem was a small town in Judah located about six miles from Jerusalem. God inspired the prophet Micah to let the people know that this was to be the birthplace of the Messiah. God chose a small, rural village, instead of the nation's capital, to manifest God's greatness. God chose the smallest Hebrew tribe, the tribe of Benjamin (see Numbers 1:35-36), to be the ancestral family in which the Messiah was raised.

The first faith lesson I want to underscore *is the surprising nature of God's activity.* God has a surprising habit of doing great things with what the world considers least or unlikely. Holy scripture bears witness repeatedly to this fact. For example, God chose David to be anointed for kingship when he was still a young boy tending sheep. David was the youngest of the eight sons of Jesse (1 Samuel 16:13). The cultural norm would have expected the eldest son rather than the youngest, but God looks not on age or stature but with the eyes of the heart.

This truth was driven home by a video I watched titled the *Tom Papania Story: From Mafia to Minister.*[1] Mr. Papania offers a moving testimonial to God's surprising grace. He grew up in an abusive home with a father who worked several jobs, drank heavily, and beat him regularly. His mother, however, was a faithful woman of prayer.

By fifteen years of age, Tom had hardened his heart against the pain and the rejection he felt from his father. He found out that his grandfather had been in the Mafia, a family secret about which his parents did not talk. Against their wishes, he rejected his family and aligned himself with these criminals, committing himself to becoming a leader in the New York Gambino crime family.

Tom pursued his life of crime with brilliance and violence. He became the third closest person to Paul Castellano, the head of the organization, and answered directly to him. Although he spent time in jail, he was always loyal to the Mafia Family. They put him in charge of restaurants, bars, gambling, prostitution, construction companies, and the like. He was bringing in tens of thousands of dollars a month. He was worth millions. He had piles of jewelry, a new Mercedes Benz, a wonderful mansion. He was highly successful at living by the law of violence, corruption, and deceit.

One factor, however, which he could not control was his mother's prayers. She prayed constantly for him, despite his separation from the family. Through a set of circumstances orchestrated by God, Tom came face to face with his own emptiness. With all his wealth and success, he felt hollow inside. In 1984, at the age of 43, having spent nearly 28 years in the Mafia, Tom had a dramatic encounter with God. God said to him, "Tom, you control all this, but you do not control me. You may think you are in charge now, but you aren't in charge of your future. You are going to hell." Having grown up in the church, Tom knew about hell. For the first time in his life, this hardened Mafia man was afraid, very afraid.

God brought him to the place of deep conviction about his sinful and debauched life. God used a country preacher to turn this man to Christ. He cut his ties with the Gambino family and survived repeated assassination attempts as a result of a $250,000 contract put out on his life. He gave away all the wealth he had accumulated and found a job. Tom's past caught up with him and he was sent to Atlanta Federal Penitentiary to await trial. The trial was one of Atlanta's longest, lasting eleven and a half months. God used the maximum security cells of the Federal prison to mold and develop a new Christ-like character for all to see. During this time, he had a face-to-face encounter with three imprisoned hit men who had been charged with eliminating him. Instead of trying to kill them, God told Tom to love these men, to forgive them, and to tell them about Jesus Christ. When he did, all three of them gave their hearts to Jesus Christ!

After almost a year, Tom was set free by the grace of God. He continued in his commitment to Christ and is now an ordained evangelist and Executive Director of "God's Saving Grace Ministries" based in Powder Springs, Georgia.

Tom Papania has been reconciled with his father. His mother got to see him once again before she died; this time it was as a Christian instead of a convict. He tours the country and the world telling thousands about what God has done for him and what God can do for them, if they will believe in Jesus Christ and accept the wonderful, surprising grace of God for themselves.

Friends, we serve a loving God who will go to surprising, extreme lengths to save his children. If God has a place in his heart to love Tom Papania (and clearly God does), then God has a place for you and me as well.

Could it be that God has been reaching out to you? Perhaps God wants to use you as God did Tom's mother, to pray unceasingly for a wayward child, family member, or friend. Let us never underestimate God's willingness to work on our behalf.

If God is putting it on your heart to pray either for yourself or another situation, I encourage you to begin praying with a trusted Christian friend. Perhaps start by meeting weekly for prayer. If meeting with another person is too difficult, why not begin praying daily and asking God to meet you at your point of greatest need?

God is willing and able to do surprising things. Prayer is often the prelude to seeing God work mightily.

Not only do people of faith encounter the surprising nature of God activity, we also experience the *hopeful nature of God's activity*. This is the second faith lesson. The prophet Isaiah declared the unflinching, unrelenting hope that following a time of national brokenness and destruction, new life would emerge. This passage is located in the second of eight volumes within the book of Isaiah and is referred to as the "Volume of Immanuel" which means "God is with us." Isaiah wrote, "There will come forth a shoot from the stump of Jesse, and a branch will grow out of his roots" (Isaiah 11:1). The image is that of a tree (in this case, a nation) which has been cut down. Nevertheless, the roots and stump are not dead. They send forth new life. When all looks hopeless on the surface, God instills deep, abiding hope.

Years of ministry have confirmed the hopeful nature of God's activity. I am amazed and gratified to see the resilience of the people of God in times of difficulty and pain. The loss of a job, the death of a loved one, a difficult or unexpected divorce, the move of a true friend, a terrible accident, a violent or abusive relationship, the failure of one's health are all examples of events which sometimes precipitate crisis, loneliness, and depression. Nevertheless, I have watched and prayed for and been encouraged as I have seen these circumstances turned by God into occasions for growth, maturation, and wisdom. With God's help, these negative experiences can be transformed into healing and restorative opportunities.

When God is at work, hope prevails against despair; love overcomes fear. When God is at work, faith conquers unbelief and trust vanquishes doubt. As long as God is at work, the weary can find rest, the restless can find peace, and the searching can find their home in Christ Jesus. Thanks be to God!

We have explored the surprising and hopeful nature of God's activity. A third faith lesson is the *contrasting nature of God's activity*. By this I mean that God works in contrasting ways with the world. During Isaiah's and Micah's time, those who ruled were often derelict in their duties. Much like our day, corruption and immorality were rampant. By contrast, Isaiah proclaimed, "The Spirit of the Lord shall rest of him, the spirit of wisdom and understanding [which is discernment and truth beneath appearances], the spirit of counsel and might [which is discretion and authority], the spirit of knowledge and the fear of the Lord [which is practical insight and reverent piety]. And his delight shall be in the fear [meaning awe] of the Lord" (Isaiah 11:2-3).

Isaiah continues, "He shall not judge by what his eyes see, or decide by what his ears hear" (Isaiah 11:3). To put it another way, this shoot from the stump will look with the eyes of the heart and his ears will search diligently until they recognize the authentic word of truth.

Reading on, "But with righteousness he shall judge the poor, and decide with equity for the meek of the earth [those who are poor and meek have a special place in the heart of God]; he shall strike the earth with the rod of his mouth [with judgment], and with the breath of his lips he shall kill the wicked [all evil will be destroyed when he appears]. Righteousness shall be the belt around his waist, and faithfulness the belt around his loins" (Isaiah 11:4-5). In other words, he will wrap himself tightly with the garments of holiness which most please God.

Isaiah's proclamation culminates in a vision of what has been termed the "peaceable kingdom." Wolf and lamb, leopard and young goat, calf and lion, child and serpent, natural enemies are brought together by the supernatural power of God. Those who were enemies are made friends. This points to the fourth faith lesson, the *reconciling nature of God's activity*. God says, "They shall not hurt or destroy in all my holy mountain; for the earth will be full of the knowledge of the Lord as the waters cover the sea" (Isaiah 11:9).

Friends, this image of a world at peace with itself, with one another and with God can only be brought about by God! The Bible says, "God was in Christ, reconciling the world to himself, not counting their trespasses against them and entrusting to us the ministry of reconciliation" (2 Corinthians 5:19). I hope that you will allow God to do this great work in you. Furthermore, may God continue this reconciling work through you until all Creation is ready and yearning for the return of Christ.

Let us pray. Lord God, we thank you for the prophets' song. We are glad that you are God, full of surprising and boundless love. We rejoice that you are the God who rekindles and inspires hope. We thank you for being a God who shines holy light into darkness and provides a bright contrast to the world. We affirm that you came in human form to reconcile us and make us new. Use the Communion that we are about to share as a means of advancing your gracious activity in our personal lives, our church, community, and world. We pray these things in the great name of our glorious and risen Savior, Jesus Christ, who has come, is now here, and is coming again. Amen.

---

1. Tom Papania, *In Search of a Father — The Tom Papania Story: From Mafia to Minister,* God's Saving Grace Ministries, P.O. Box 756, Powder Springs, Georgia 30127. Phone: (770) 590-8775, Fax: (770) 590-0130. Used with permission.

Celebrating The Lord's Day
Third Sunday Of Advent

Opening Sentence Luke 1:46-48, The Message
Mary said, "I am bursting with Good News; I'm dancing the song of my Savior God. God took one good look at me, and look what happened — I'm the most fortunate woman on earth!"

Greetings
We are blessed that you have chosen to worship with us today! May the living God draw near you today and touch you at your point of deepest need.

Parish Announcements

Prelude Suggestions
Glory To God In The Highest G. Pergolesi
Angels We Have Heard On High arr. F. Bock

Choral Introit Come, Thou Long Expected Jesus
R. Prichard

*Call To Worship Luke 1:46-48a, 50 CEV
Leader: With all my heart I praise the Lord.
People: And I am glad because of God my Savior.
Leader: God cares for me, his humble servant.
People: God always shows mercy to everyone who worships him.

*Processional Hymn There's A Song In The Air

*Welcome One Another
Please greet those around you and introduce yourself to two persons you do not know by name.

Advent Candle Lighting Ceremony[1]
Leader: Christ came to bring us salvation and has promised to come again. Let us pray that we may always be ready to welcome him. (*Light the first candle*)
People: Come, Lord Jesus.
Leader: That the keeping of Advent may open our hearts to God's love. (*Light the second candle*)
People: Come, Lord Jesus.
Leader: That the light of Christ may penetrate the darkness of sin. (*Light the third candle*)
People: Come, Lord Jesus.
Leader: We light these candles as a symbol of Christ, our comfort and hope whom God has given to us.
**All: Lord God,
your Church joyfully awaits the coming of its Savior,
who enlightens our hearts
and dispels the darkness of ignorance and sin.**

**Pour forth your blessings upon us
as we light the candles of this wreath.
May their light reflect the splendor of Christ,
who is Lord, for ever and ever. Amen.**

Children's Message

Anthem   The First Noel/Pachelbel's Canon
                                                                              M. Clawson

Call To Prayer
(*Everyone singing, O Little Town Of Bethlehem*)
   **How silently, how silently the wondrous gift is given; so God imparts to human hearts the blessings of his heaven.
   No ear may hear his coming, but in this world of sin, where meek souls will receive him, still the dear Christ enters in.**

Collect

Mighty God, you have made us and all things to serve you. We need your guidance as to how to live faithfully. We need you to illumine our minds to understand and accept the paradoxical ways you work in this world. Draw near to us. Teach us. Encourage us. May our faith grow and become a strong and unshakable witness to your love and power. We ask these things through Jesus our Lord who lives and reigns with you and with the Holy Spirit, one God, forever. Amen.

Morning Prayer And Lord's Prayer

Our Father, who art in heaven, hallowed be thy name. Thy kingdom come; thy will be done on earth as it is in heaven. Give us this day our daily bread. And forgive us our trespasses, as we forgive those who trespass against us. And lead us not into temptation, but deliver us from evil. For thine is the kingdom, and the power, and the glory, forever. Amen.

Giving Of Tithes And Offerings

Offertory Suggestion
 Gloria   A. Vivaldi

*Presentation Response   Doxology
Praise God from whom all blessings flow; praise him all creatures here below; praise him above ye heavenly host; praise Father, Son and Holy Ghost. Amen.

*Prayer Of Dedication

Old Testament: Isaiah 40:1-5
Leader: God always blesses the reading of the Word.
People: Lord, open our hearts to you.

*Gospel: Luke 1:46-55
(or "Canticle of Mary" from the *United Methodist Hymnal* No. 199 with sung response. This hymn text is taken from Luke 1:46b-55)

Leader: This is the Gospel of our Lord.
People: Thanks be to God.

Sermon   Mary's Song
Part three in the series, *Songs For A Savior*

*Hymn   My Soul Gives Glory To My God

*Blessing

*Choral Response   Rejoice
                                                     13th Century Plainsong

*Postlude   Glory To God
                                                              Z. Harbro

* * * * *

*All who are able are invited to stand.

---

1. Advent candle lighting ceremony adapted from "Blessings of the Advent Wreath" from the *Book of Blessings*, additional blessings for use in the United States of America © 1988 United States Conference of Catholic Bishops, Inc., Washington, D.C. Used with permission. All rights reserved. No portion of this text may be reproduced by any means without permission in writing from the copyright holder.

Mary's Song
Part three in the series: **Songs For A Savior**
Third Sunday Of Advent

Isaiah 40:1-5; Luke 1:46-55

During Advent we are exploring what it means to live faithfully as we prepare to celebrate the birth of Jesus and to await the return of Christ our Savior. Our theme for Advent and Christmas is "Songs For A Savior." Today we examine "Mary's Song" and what it says to us about God's paradoxical values.

A paradox is something that appears to be contradictory but is, in fact, true. Human beings often struggle with paradox. We would be so much happier if life were straightforward and delivered to us in ways we could plainly understand. But God's ways are often surprising, especially to those who are very certain that God can only act in one particular way. We certainly see such surprises in Mary's encounter with the angel Gabriel and in her response to his announcement that she was chosen by God to give birth to the Savior of the world.

Mary's encounter with God reveals three paradoxes which give important insights into how God acted in Mary's day as well as how God works today. First is the paradox of *humble origins*. It would have made sense to the Jews of Jesus' day, as it would make sense to us, if Jesus had been born to intellectuals who were powerful religious leaders in Jerusalem. If this had occurred, Jesus would have grown up in the rarified atmosphere of the spiritual and intellectual elite. God had worked that way before in Moses' life and in the lives of some of the prophets.

It would have made sense to most people if the Messiah, the Savior of the world, had been born into a household where he would have been comfortably sheltered and given the best of everything. The announcement by Gabriel to Mary, however, occurred in Nazareth of Galilee. No one expected that the Messiah would come from such a place (John 7:41). As far back as the time of the prophet Isaiah, Galilee was seen as a place of spiritual darkness.

Many who lived in Galilee made their livelihood from the commercial traffic which passed through the region. The main north-south highway, the Via Maris, the Way of the Sea, went through this land. Jews would normally shun contact with outsiders, but many Galileans relied on trade with the caravans to earn a living. As such, these Jews were seen as second class, as spiritually deficient compromisers who walked in darkness because of their dealings with non-Jews.

Paradoxically, Galilee was named by Isaiah as the place where God's light would shine brightly. Isaiah 9:1b-2 declares, "... he will make glorious the way of the sea, the land beyond the Jordan, Galilee of the nations. The people who walked in darkness have seen a great light; those who lived in a land of deep darkness — on them light has shined." This passage reflects the mysterious paradox of God choosing a place of spiritual darkness and moral decline to shine divine light and proclaim good news. It reflects God's priorities and foreshadows Jesus' ministry with the least, the last, and the lost. God seems to be in the habit of doing remarkable things through humble people of humble origins. God selected a region that was considered "least" to be given the exalted position of being the home of the Messiah.

How might this paradox of humble origins address you and me? Too often we focus on outward things. We use the superficial values of the world to decide whether a person or a place is of worth. God does not seem to be impressed with the outward trappings of success or achievement. God looks on the heart. God sees with the eyes of faith. God knows whether or not a person will be loyal. God trusts and blesses accordingly. Instead of seeing someone's humble birth as a liability, God values it. In the sight of God, humility is a strength. People of faith must be willing to ask for God's perception, for God's values, as they live and work and relate to others. We must not assume that the word and the world view of the powerful or the educated are more important than the word and the world of those who are less advantaged. We must ask God's help to see with the eyes of faith.

The second paradox is *favored status*. We normally think of someone being favored because they have a special position. We give favored status to dignitaries and VIPs — Very Important Persons. These people are usually ascribed this status because they have power, influence, or money. In contrast, the Gospel of Luke shows Mary being told of her favored status by the angel Gabriel. Gabriel said, "Greetings, favored one! The Lord is with you." Mary was not accustomed to being addressed in such a way. The Bible says, "She was much perplexed by [Gabriel's] words and pondered what sort of greeting this might be" (Luke 1:29).

The Gospel writer continues, "The angel said to her, 'Do not be afraid, Mary, for you have found favor with God' " (Luke 1:30). Not only was Mary surprised by the visitation of the great archangel Gabriel she was confused by his bestowing favored status upon her. She was a Jewish girl from a poor family and probably only about twelve years of age. As such, she had such a low social status that it ranked just above those who were non-Jews. What had she done which deserved special status in the eyes of the Living God? The answer is nothing, at least nothing that can be explicitly found in scripture. *The favor God bestowed upon Mary was not earned; it was a gift of God.* God decided to grace her and bless her with the awesome privilege and responsibility of bearing the Son of God.

Unearned favor is difficult for us to comprehend. We are used to thinking in terms of rewards and consequences. We believe that hard work is to be recognized and rewarded, while a job poorly done deserves criticism and consequences. We believe this system of recognition or rebuke rests on *our* effort and *our* persistence. Mary's life shows us a different way.

The paradox of unearned favor is central to our faith. It gives us hope when we fail. It enables us to continue to seek God when we find ourselves outside of God's will. Unearned favor empowers us to open up the deepest part of our hearts and helps us to trust again. God knows us through and through. God is willing, despite what he knows to be true about us, to love us and to welcome us into his presence. This is an awesome gift and a holy paradox. If we can embrace this reality, it can help us return to God and find our home and our resting place in the Lord.

Ask yourself, "Where would I be today if God had not bestowed on me unearned favor?" As you ponder this, I hope that you will be drawn to offer yourself — heart, soul, mind, and strength to serve Almighty God and to receive and honor Jesus Christ as your Lord and Savior. The One who bestows unearned favor upon us is certainly worthy of *our* favor, love, and trust.

We have explored the paradoxes of humble origins and favored status. The third paradox we find in this Gospel narrative is the paradox of *vulnerability*. God could have come into the world in any form. Amazingly, Almighty God came in the vulnerability of a helpless baby. Furthermore, the all-powerful God went in search of a faithful, young woman who would give her assent to this miraculous plan for the salvation of the world. God became vulnerable and awaited the consent of Mary. True love waits in vulnerability and trust. True love waits for the willing consent of the other.

In addition to God's vulnerability, we also see in this account the vulnerability of Mary. God sought a woman who would conceive and nurture the Savior of the world in her womb at the risk of her reputation and her life. Jewish law indicated that a woman who was not found to be a virgin could be stoned to death. If a betrothed virgin such as Mary were to have sex with another man and it was discovered, the law indicated that both should be stoned to death according to Deuteronomy 22:20-27. Mary risked everything, her life and all her worldly security, when she said, "Here am I, the servant of the Lord; let it be with me according to your word" (Luke 1:38). She trusted that God was loving. She embraced the vulnerability required to respond to God's call. God blessed it and made her amazingly strong and faithful.

How much have we allowed ourselves to be vulnerable for the sake of honoring and obeying God? Have we been willing to face criticism or misunderstanding? Have we been willing to risk the respect of family, friends, or the community? Have we ever put our faith on the line and stood up for what we have believed? What has our belief in Christ cost?

Vulnerability is something many try to avoid. In this passage, however, we find every reason to embrace vulnerability. Through both God's vulnerability and Mary's vulnerability, the world received the gift of the Savior. Vulnerability makes us more God-dependent, more God-reliant rather than self-reliant. In the end, vulnerability makes us strong. Godly vulnerability empowers us to follow the Lord in faith, rather than pursuing self-made security; it opens us to God's priorities and values. Vulnerability helps us to understand that we are not here to satisfy ourselves but to serve God.

The question is *not*, "What do I want; what would make me happy?" The question which vulnerability keeps raising is, "What do you want, O God? What would please you? How do you want me to honor you and lay down my life?" Such questions may be new or uncommon for you to ask. They are, however, faithful questions and reflect a correct attitude and approach to the Christian life. Living these questions will help to turn our upside down world, right side up, so that the kingdom of God may come and God's will be done here in this community and within our congregation.

Listen for the paradoxes of humble origins, favored status, and vulnerability as found in Luke's Gospel as you hear again the song of Mary:

> *My soul magnifies the Lord, and my spirit rejoices in God my Savior, for he has looked with favor on the lowliness of his servant. Surely, from now on all generations will call me blessed; for the Mighty One has done great things for me, and holy is his name. His mercy is for those who fear him from generation to generation. He has shown strength with his arm; he has scattered the proud in the thoughts of their hearts. He has brought down the powerful from their thrones, and lifted up the lowly; he has filled the hungry with good things, and sent the rich away empty. He has helped his servant Israel, in remembrance of his mercy, according to the promise he made to our ancestors, to Abraham and to his descendants forever.* — Luke 1:46-55

Those who know God and God's grace are called to echo Mary's song. Although we do not have the honor of giving birth to the Savior of the world, we are given the privilege of following him and leading others to do the same. The paradoxes of God are as real today as they were when Mary was approached by the angel.

God wants you and me to be involved in God's work. What a joy! What a magnificent blessing! Thanks be to God!

Let us pray. O God, we wonder about your ways and we are in awe of your greatness. Your values are full of paradox. They make us uncomfortable because we are so used to living by the standards of the world. Yet you still call to us. You seek us out and reveal another way to live, a much better way to live. You challenge us to embrace your truth, the truth that will abide, the truth that will sustain. Help us discover the strength that comes when we are vulnerable before you, O God. Teach us to welcome and accept your favored status. May we always live in humility, grateful for your bountiful gifts to us. In Jesus' name, we pray. Amen.

Celebrating The Lord's Day
Fourth Sunday Of Advent

Opening Sentence   Luke 2:15
"When the angels went away from them into heaven, the shepherds said to one another, 'Let us go over to Bethlehem and see this thing that has happened, which the Lord has made known to us.'"

Greetings
We are blessed that you have chosen to worship with us today! May the living God draw near to you today and touch you at your point of deepest need.

Parish Announcements

Prelude Suggestions
   Joyous Proclamation   arr. S. Caudill
   Christmas Fanfare   arr. S. Caudill

Choral Introit   O Come, All Ye Faithful
                                                     R. Koury

*Call To Worship   Luke 2:10-12
Leader: I am bringing you good news of great joy for all the people.
All: (*singing*) **O come, all ye faithful, joyful and triumphant, O come ye, O come ye, to Bethlehem.**
Leader: To you is born this day in the city of David a Savior who is the Messiah, the Lord.
All: (*singing*) **Come and behold him, born the King of angels.**
Leader: You will find a child wrapped in bands of cloth and lying in a manger.
All: (*singing*) **O come, let us adore him; O come, let us adore him; O come, let us adore him, Christ the Lord.**

*Processional Hymn O Come, All Ye Faithful
(vv. 2-6)

*Welcome One Another
Please greet those around you and introduce yourself to two persons you do not know by name.

Advent Candle Lighting Ceremony[1]
Leader: Christ came to bring us salvation and has promised to come again. Let us pray that we may always be ready to welcome him. (*Light the first candle*)
People: Come, Lord Jesus.
Leader: That the keeping of Advent may open our hearts to God's love. (*Light the second candle*)
People: Come, Lord Jesus.
Leader: That the light of Christ may penetrate the darkness of sin. (*Light the third candle*)
People: Come, Lord Jesus.
Leader: That this wreath may constantly remind us to prepare for the coming of Christ. (*Light the fourth candle*)
People: Come, Lord Jesus.
Leader: Four Advent candles are lighted in expectation of the return of Christ, our Savior and Lord, whom God has given to us.
All: Lord God,
your Church joyfully awaits the coming of its Savior,
who enlightens our hearts
and dispels the darkness of ignorance and sin.

Pour forth your blessings upon us
as we light the candles of this wreath.
May their light reflect the splendor of Christ,
who is Lord, for ever and ever. Amen.

Children's Message

Anthem Suggestions
    Carol For Advent   Price/Besig
    Gesu Bambino   P. A. Yon

Collect
Lord, help us to remember the wonder of Christmas: the wonder we experienced as children when we could hardly wait for that great day; the wonder of knowing your amazing power as experienced by Mary and Joseph; the wonder of hearing the story of your love that thrilled the hearts of the shepherds. We thank and praise you for the love you have given us in Jesus. In his name, we pray. Amen.

Morning Prayer And Lord's Prayer
Our Father, who art in heaven, hallowed be thy name. Thy kingdom come; thy will be done on earth as it is in heaven. Give us this day our daily bread. And forgive us our trespasses, as we forgive those who trespass against us. And lead us not into temptation, but deliver us from evil. For thine is the kingdom, and the power, and the glory, forever. Amen.

Giving Of Tithes And Offerings

Offertory   Jesu Bambino
                                                                                  Yore

*Presentation Response   Emmanuel, Emmanuel

*Prayer Of Dedication

*Gospel: Luke 2:8-20
Leader: This is the Gospel of our Lord.
People: **Thanks be to God.**

Sermon   The Songs Of The Angels And Shepherds
Part four in the series, *Songs For A Savior*

*Hymn   Angels We Have Heard On High

*Blessing

*Choral Response

*Postlude Suggestions
  Caroling, Caroling   arr. Bish
  Joy To The World   arr. F. Bock

* * * * *

*All who are able are invited to stand.

---

1. Advent candle lighting ceremony adapted from "Blessings of the Advent Wreath" from the *Book of Blessings*, additional blessings for use in the United States of America © 1988 United States Conference of Catholic Bishops, Inc., Washington, D.C. Used with permission. All rights reserved. No portion of this text may be reproduced by any means without permission in writing from the copyright holder.

The Songs Of The Angels And Shepherds
Part four in the series: Songs For A Savior
Fourth Sunday Of Advent

Luke 2:8-20

During the weeks of Advent, we have been exploring what it means to live faithfully as we prepare to celebrate the birth of Jesus as well as await the return of Christ, our Savior. We have drawn insight from the Old and New Testaments as we have discussed "Zechariah's Song," "The Prophets' Song," and "Mary's Song." Today we explore "The Songs Of The Angels And Shepherds."

As I examined the Gospel lesson, I was drawn to five responses made by the different characters in Luke's nativity narrative. These reactions are illustrative of ones you and I might have to such a story. As you listen to each, think about how you have responded in the past and how you would like to respond to God's activity today.

The first response is *exclamation* as illustrated by the exclamation of angels. God sent an angel to shepherds outside Bethlehem. We are not told explicitly, but the angel could have been the archangel Gabriel who figures prominently and is mentioned by Luke in two earlier stories (see Luke 1:19, 26).

The angel was filled with joy. He exclaimed that he had been sent to bring the shepherds "good news of great joy." His heavenly announcement concerned the earthly birth of God's long-awaited Messiah, the Savior of the world (Luke 2:10-11). This was world-class news! God was fulfilling a centuries-awaited promise to all humanity!

So dynamic and important was this news that suddenly there was with the angel a multitude of the heavenly host, praising God and saying, "Glory to God in the highest heaven, and on earth peace among those whom he favors" (Luke 2:14). It was as if these angelic beings were bursting with joy! They could not contain themselves. Their exclamations of praise filled the air with a Hallelujah Chorus of heavenly music.

Think about a time when you were filled with exuberant, good news that you could hardly contain. Was it the birth of a child or grandchild? Was it a beautiful surprise or an unexpected visit from loved ones? When we have powerful good news, we cannot help but share it. The words come bursting from our lips with excitement, joy, and a deep sense of gratitude.

I invite you to pray that this exuberance will be a part of your Christian life and faith. Let God fill you with overflowing joy so that a song of praise will burst from your heart and be formed on your lips. Such exuberance, such an exclamation of praise in one's life is readily apparent. People see and are drawn to this contagious Christianity.

Having been awestruck by the exclamation of the angels, *surprise* is the next response, as demonstrated in the surprise of the shepherds over the birth announcement of God's Son. At first, the shepherds were fearfully surprised by the appearance of the angel, the heavenly host, and the glorious light of God's presence shining around them. This did not last, however. So incredible was this experience and so great was the power of the good news that the *surprise of fear* turned to the *surprise of wonder*!

As their fear waned, their curiosity mounted. The shepherds decided to act on the announcement. Having heard the exclamation of the angels and experienced the surprise of fear and wonder, these shepherds could not go back to business as usual. They were not satisfied to hear the testimony of the heavenly host. They had to experience God's good news for themselves. Secondhand information would not satisfy. They needed to test the trustworthiness of the announcement. They had to confirm the vision. They said, " 'Let us go now to Bethlehem to see this thing that has taken place, which the Lord has made known to us.' So they went with haste and found ... the child lying in the manger" (Luke 2:15-16).

We can readily identify with the shepherds and with Mary and Joseph before them. Our first emotion is often to feel afraid or overwhelmed when we are surprised in new and unfamiliar ways. Perhaps you can recall a time when God surprised you. How did you react? What did you feel? Was your initial response fear, followed by a gradual emergence of peace? Did your surprise turn to joy?

As a pastor, people have shared with me many different moments when God has come close to them in unexpected ways. Some years ago an elderly person shared with me about how she had been sick for several months. As she rested in bed one evening, it was as if the room filled with light. A strong, heavenly figure stood at the foot of her bed and called her by name. She was startled and afraid at first. She thought that perhaps her time had come to die. Instead, the heavenly being spoke to her and reassured her that her prayers were being answered, not only concerning her own illness, but also for her family members who had not yet given their lives to Jesus Christ. The end result was that this startling, surprising experience turned into a deep, peaceful reassurance. She knew that God was with her and was listening to her prayers. As a result, she prayed more fervently. Her faith became powerful and comforting to many others. She became an even more radiant witness for and effective disciple of Jesus Christ.

Perhaps you know of someone who has had a similar experience. Maybe you recall a time in your own life when some powerful, unexpected good news was announced to you. Did you have a hard time believing it? Did you exclaim, "That is unbelievable! Are you sure?" In times such as this, our disbelief turns to joy. Our surprise turns to celebration. We know, beyond a shadow of a doubt, that God has been at work. We feel exceedingly blessed. We are reassured of God's providential care and goodness. These are some of the emotions the shepherds must have felt that night long ago.

We have discussed the exclamation of the angels and the surprise of the shepherds. The third response is *amazement*, amazement on the part of the townspeople at the announcement of the shepherds. The shepherds went in search of the Son of God whom they were told could be found wrapped in bands of cloth and lying in a manger. In the middle of the night, they scoured the nearby village of Bethlehem. They were relentless in their search. At last, they found the holy family with the baby Jesus in the manger. It was just as they had been told. Luke reports: "When they saw this, they made known what had been told them about this child; and all who heard it were amazed at what the shepherds told them" (Luke 2:17-18).

I am amazed at God's choice of persons to announce the birth of his son. The shepherds were considered among the least, the last, and the lost of society. Shepherds were held in such ill repute that their testimony was not allowed in a court of law. They were viewed as social outcasts, as spiritually bankrupt, as unlearned and uncouth. They were known as scoundrels, cheats, and liars. Amazingly, God chose to give those whom society considered as having nothing of value to share the greatest news ever heard by human ears.

Furthermore, the good news of the Messiah's birth not only inspired the shepherds, it affected all those who heard their testimony. Even though some may have questioned or doubted the witness of the shepherds, no one dismissed the news casually. Amazement filled them all as the people of Bethlehem heard what had happened and what the angels had proclaimed to the shepherds.

When were you amazed? Think back to a time when you stood in awe and wonder. Was it a natural setting such as the immense power and roar of Niagara Falls or the vast beauty and depth of the Grand Canyon? Was it an experience you had while watching a movie, reading a book, listening to a symphony, or going to an outstanding play? Was it visiting some great monument or standing before an architectural wonder? Perhaps it was watching or reading about a great accomplishment, such as climbing Mount Everest or a physician performing a pioneering operation. Many parents speak of the profound amazement and humbling awe they feel at the miracle of each child's birth.

We live in an age of cynicism and doubt. We need experiences of amazement. Amazement gives perspective, rearranges and broadens narrow realities, and defies our common expectations. Amazement is a gift sorely needed by both young and old. It makes us aware of the heavenly breaking into the earthly, the eternal penetrating the temporal, the divine infusing the mundane.

Life is enriched by amazement. Look for it. Expect it. Pray for it. You will be greatly touched and forever blessed in such a quest. We serve an amazing God who continues to act in amazing ways.

When you experience something amazing, I encourage you not to hesitate to share. Tell your good news. Be bold as the shepherds were. If necessary, shout it out! The world needs more amazement.

Mary had a different response than the amazement of the townspeople. Luke says, "... Mary treasured all these words and pondered them in her heart" (Luke 2:19). The fourth response is *pondering*, as evidenced by the pondering of Mary.

Webster's dictionary defines *ponder* as follows: "to consider something deeply and thoroughly; meditate; to weigh carefully in the mind."[1] Sometimes the deepest reaction to a profound or amazing experience is a quiet, inward, subdued response. For example, when I have heard a glorious, stirring piece of music, my first inclination is not always to applaud but to ponder, to reflect, to give thanks inwardly. I want to savor the moment. I want to linger there awhile. I want the emotion, the incredible power, the awe of the moment to soak in and become part of me. Applause, rather than extending the sense of reverie and gratitude, can sometimes interrupt it.

Mary chose to ponder the announcement given by the shepherds. In addition to being exhausted from giving birth to her firstborn, she may have needed time to be quiet, to try to make sense of what was being said. So many strange things had taken place in the recent past. She had been told by the angel Gabriel, nine months previously, that she would have a child by the Holy Spirit of God. This child's destiny had been disclosed to her at that time:

> ... *you will conceive in your womb and bear a son, and you will name him Jesus. He will be great, and will be called the Son of the Most High, and the Lord God will give to him the throne of his ancestor David. He will reign over the house of Jacob forever, and of his kingdom there will be no end.* — Luke 1:31-33

Mary was a peasant girl from a poor family. She was a far cry from royalty. She had no access to the power structures of the day. Nevertheless, the announcement of Gabriel and the testimony of the shepherds pointed to her infant child being the Son of God, a ruler whose kingdom would be like great King David's. Of his kingdom, there would be no end. It was more than she could grasp.

A borrowed stable and feed trough for a bed were surely an inauspicious beginning for someone purportedly of divine destiny. Pondering was certainly an understandable and suitable response.

We live in an age in which we are constantly bombarded with noise. Sights and sounds relentlessly grab our attention. Some people have the television or radio on from morning until bedtime. They say they keep it on for company. Time for silent pondering is greatly needed. When we take time to ponder in the silence, we open ourselves to new insight. We are rewarded in our search for deeper meaning. Our quest for understanding and truth is frequently the fruit of pondering. Pondering helps us to soak in the life-giving, loving presence of God who is with us always but who is crowded out when our life becomes too busy and too noisy.

If you are not used to taking time to ponder, I encourage you to begin with ten minutes of quiet a day. Remove yourself from distractions. Turn off the offending noise. Go to a room by yourself. Be still. Breathe deeply a few times. Invite God into your stillness. Offer to the Lord the things which concern you and ask for God to give you divine perspective. If you will do this daily for just one month, you may discover what others have experienced. Pondering will become a necessity instead of an oddity. It will be vital for you because you will have a new, deeper sense of being in touch with the living God. Try it. You have nothing to lose and much to gain.

One final response remains to be explored briefly. In addition to the exclamation of angels, the surprise of shepherds, the amazement of the townspeople, and the pondering of Mary, the fifth response is *celebration*, the celebration of the shepherds. Luke says, "The shepherds returned, glorifying and praising God for all they had heard and seen, as it had been told them" (Luke 2:20).

When something great happens, it is cause for celebration. Celebration serves to mark significant moments. We celebrate birthdays, anniversaries, and graduations. We set aside holidays so as to have adequate, collective time to remember and give thanks for great events in our past as a country and as people of faith. We put up special decorations, get together with significant family and friends, and prepare favorite foods. Do we need to do this in order to have a holiday? No. The day would be a holiday whether we observed it or not. However, it is much more meaningful when we take the time to make a special observance of the day.

Celebrations enable us to remember and to give thanks. Celebrations remind us of our heritage. They give us an important center, a sense of being grounded. They help us to reorder our life and priorities. They cause us to step back and reflect. Celebrations add a richness and depth to our lives which all of us need from time to time.

The shepherds returned from finding Jesus, God's Messiah, with celebration bubbling up in their hearts. They marked this significant time by talking about it excitedly. They reveled in the memory of the day when the angels visited them in the fields. They rejoiced that God came to them and announced the good news to them personally. Although they were the lowest caste of society, they were privileged to share the greatest news of history, God becoming flesh.

It seems fitting that God's great, good news was announced by both the least of society and by the host of heaven. I do not believe it is a coincidence that this child was announced by human as well as heavenly beings. Christians believe that Jesus was fully human and fully divine. Therefore, it seems appropriate that this dual announcement was celebrated by the earthly and heavenly creation.

How will you celebrate the birth of Christ? Will there be time in your schedule to rejoice in him? Will you mark this sacred occasion by more than brightly wrapped packages and good food?

My prayer is that you will make room for whatever response to God's gift of Jesus that is most necessary at this time in your life. Just as God reached out to humanity 2,000 ago, may you discover God reaching to you in this holy season of Christmas. May the exclamation of the angels, the surprise of the shepherds, the amazement of the townspeople, the pondering of Mary, and the celebration of the shepherds become part of your holy days this year.

Let us pray. Most gracious, kind, understanding, and loving God, we thank you for coming among us, being born in human flesh, and showing us how to live. Thank you for the many positive responses we can legitimately have to your coming. Draw near to us in this holy time. Enrich our lives with your extraordinary presence as you did ordinary people long ago. We ask these things in the name of Christ, your Son and our Savior. Amen.

---

1. *Webster's New Universal Unabridged Dictionary* (New York: Barnes and Noble Books, 1994).

The Festival Of The Holy Nativity
Christmas Eve

Prelude Organ Suggestions
    Joy To The World   arr. Petker
    O Come, All Ye Faithful   arr. Burroughs
    Silent Night   arr. Bock
    The First Noel   arr. McKecknie

Trumpet
    Carol Medley   arr. Hamilton

Handbell Choir
    The Holly And The Ivy   Christmas Carillon

Organ, Piano, And Keyboard
    Oh, Come All Ye Faithful   arr. Billingsley

Flute
    Angels We Have Heard On High   arr. Schuster
    O Come, O Come, Immanuel   arr. Schuster

Organ
    Hark! The Herald Angels Sing   Mendelssohn

Welcome
    Merry Christmas to each of you! We are honored to have you join us for this special occasion of celebration.

Call To Worship   Luke 2:10-11
    "I am bringing you good news of great joy for all the people: to you is born this day in the city of David a Savior, who is the Messiah, the Lord."

Procession Of The Carols
    Please remain seated as we sing the first verse of each carol from memory.
        O Come, All Ye Faithful   John F. Wade
        O Little Town Of Bethlehem   Phillips Brooks

Joy To The World — Isaac Watts
It Came Upon The Midnight Clear — Edmund H. Sears
The First Noel — Trad. English Carol

The Lighting Of The Christ Candle[1]

Leader: Christ came to bring us salvation and has promised to come again. Let us pray that we may always be ready to welcome him. (*Light the first candle*)

People: Come, Lord Jesus.

Leader: That the keeping of Advent may open our hearts to God's love. (*Light the second candle*)

People: Come, Lord Jesus.

Leader: That the light of Christ may penetrate the darkness of sin. (*Light the third candle*)

People: Come, Lord Jesus.

Leader: That this wreath may constantly remind us to prepare for the coming of Christ. (*Light the fourth candle*)

People: Come, Lord Jesus.

Leader: That the Christmas season may fill us with peace and joy as we strive to follow the example of Jesus. (*Light the Christ Candle*)

People: Come, Lord Jesus.

Leader: These candles have been lit as a symbol of Christ, our Savior, whom God has given to us in love.

**All: Lord God,
your Church joyfully awaits the coming of its Savior,
who enlightens our hearts
and dispels the darkness of ignorance and sin.**

**Pour forth your blessings upon us
as we light the candles of this wreath.
May their light reflect the splendor of Christ,
who is Lord, for ever and ever. Amen.**

Old Testament: Isaiah 9:2-7

Leader: This is the Word of the Lord.

People: Thanks be to God.

Anthem
    Angel's Carol   John Rutter

*Gospel: Luke 2:1-7
Leader: This is the Gospel of our Lord.
People: Praise be to you, Lord Jesus Christ. Amen.

Anthem
    Away In The Manger   Paul Sjoland

Christmas Meditation   Our Song For The Savior
    Part five in the series, *Songs For A Savior*

Giving Our Gifts In Adoration Of Christ Jesus

Offertory Anthem
    O Holy Night

Candle Lighting Ceremony
    We will remain seated throughout the candle lighting ceremony. The young women will bring the light to those at the end of the pews. Always keep your lighted candles upright and tip the unlighted candles as you pass the light along your row. Please watch that no clothing or hair gets near the flame. For your safety, ushers will be in the outside aisles with fire extinguishers and damp towels. Our recommendation is that children less than sixth grade share a candle with a parent or adult. Please extinguish your candle following the Lord's Prayer but take the light of Christ that is in you into the world.

Anthem Or Hymn Suggestions
    I Want To Walk As A Child Of The Light
    Shine The Light Of Your Love   Patterson

Carol By Candlelight
    Silent Night   Joseph Mohr

(*The organist will play through Silent Night once, then all are invited to join in singing.*[2] *Carefully raise your lighted candles during the third stanza as a tribute to God's Wondrous Light, Jesus Christ, shining in our lives and through us to the world.*)

Benediction And Lord's Prayer
(*You are invited to pray in unison with your eyes open.*)
   Our Father, who art in heaven, hallowed be thy name. Thy kingdom come; thy will be done on earth as it is in heaven. Give us this day our daily bread. And forgive us our trespasses, as we forgive those who trespass against us. And lead us not into temptation, but deliver us from evil. For thine is the kingdom, and the power, and the glory, forever. Amen.

Extinguishing Of The Candles

*Postlude
   Carols Of Christmas   Doran
(*The organist should select something quiet to perpetuate the mood of people leaving with a deep sense of peace and the presence of God.*)

* * * * *

*All who are able are invited to stand.

---

1. Advent candle lighting ceremony adapted from "Blessings of the Advent Wreath" from the *Book of Blessings*, additional blessings for use in the United States of America © 1988 United States Conference of Catholic Bishops, Inc., Washington, D.C. Used with permission. All rights reserved. No portion of this text may be reproduced by any means without permission in writing from the copyright holder.

2. The four verses of the carol may be printed in the bulletin or on a bulletin insert.

Our Song For The Savior
Part five in the series, *Songs For A Savior*
Christmas Eve

Isaiah 9:2-7; Luke 2:1-20

During the weeks of Advent leading up to Christmas, we have been exploring what it means to live faithfully as we prepare to celebrate the birth of Jesus and as we await the return of Christ, our Savior. We have drawn insight from the scriptures as reflected in "Zechariah's Song," "The Prophet's Song," "Mary's Song," and "The Songs Of The Angels And Shepherds."

In these familiar accounts, we have seen that faithful people have a song to sing as a result of an encounter with God or the announcement of Jesus' birth. We have also seen that the song of celebration does not always begin immediately. In most cases, the first response is to be startled or afraid, to have a sense of awe, wonder, and amazement.

Tonight's reading of the birth story in Luke portrays this very clearly. The shepherds were afraid at first. Fear, however, turned to wonder and amazement. Wonder and amazement turned to curiosity. Curiosity turned to action. Action resulted in the search for and discovery of Mary, Joseph, and the child in the manger. Discovery gave way to rejoicing and sharing the good news the angels had told them. Good news overcame and overcomes fear. Hope is victorious over uncertainty and doubt.

In our lives, we can identify with this range of emotions and responses. Along with our sisters and brothers in the faith before us, we too struggle to make sense of what God is doing and how God is working. Fear, sorrow, frustration, and anger may rise to the surface of our lives in response to pain and difficulty. Another emotion is also frequently present: the sense of comfort and the inner assurance that we are not alone.

I will never forget when one of my colleagues in the ministry, a person with whom I worked and for whom many had prayed during her problem pregnancy, gave birth to a stillborn son on Christmas Eve. God's answer to our prayers was difficult to accept. It was a painful time for many, especially those closest to my grieving friend. One thing all of us experienced that night, however, was the sense of God being with us. God was with the grieving couple and their families. God was with us in our loss. We all had a sense of God's comfort, love, and grace.

Who of us has not struggled with discerning where and how God is at work when a loved one has an accident or gets seriously ill and dies, when a friend is beaten or abused, or when a spouse decides to leave the marriage? These are the common experiences of humanity. We struggle to hear God's song at times such as these. Nevertheless, God is with us. God walks with us throughout the journey of life.

Fortunately, there are also other times of great joy, times when the Lord seems so clearly present and seems to answer our prayers in ways beyond what we can ask for or even imagine. I have asked a member of our congregation to share a small portion of her story with us this evening.

(Pastors are invited to have someone in their congregation offer a personal testimony here. The one that follows is used with permission and may be incorporated into your message if that is desired.)

Lisa Fisher's Testimony:
Over the years I have struggled to walk the walk and to talk the talk of true faith. Just going through the motions without the heartfelt commitment was not satisfying. Although many years ago I asked God into my heart, it was not until recently that I really experienced the personal touch of God. Some of you know that over the past couple of years, I have had Achilles tendon surgery and subsequent other problems requiring that I use crutches. The doctor put me back into a cast to see if it would help. If it did not, I was told that I would require another surgery.

It was twelve weeks ago that my Bible Study class prayed over me. They gathered around me while I sat in a chair. They laid their hands upon me and prayed for my healing. As we sought the Lord together, I asked Jesus Christ to heal me if that was in his plan for me. As we continued in prayer, I felt a warm sensation start in my feet and it flowed through my whole body. I experienced the touch of God's Spirit. When I arose from the chair that evening I knew that I had been healed. To confirm it, the doctors cut the cast off my leg a few days later. I have been pain free ever since. I praise God for caring enough for me to touch me in this wonderful way. I sense a new song in my heart, a song of joy and thanksgiving for all he has done for me.

Have you ever seen the twinkle of pride in a parent's eye when their child has done something outstanding? Tonight, as your candles are lighted, think of the love which our Heavenly Father has for each of us. The best present you can open this Christmas isn't lying under a tree; it is a gift paid for and given to you by your Heavenly Father. God gave the gift of his Son so that all humanity could be set free from sin, enjoy peace with one another, and hope for eternity. God wants Jesus Christ to be born this night in each of our hearts. I invite you to open your heart to him and let his light shine on you and through you to bless others.

Thank you, Lisa, for sharing with us. We appreciate your willingness to share this wonderful news of God's loving, healing touch in your life.

No matter what you and I are experiencing in life at this moment, the absolute truth is — God cares. God, our Creator, knows us completely and loves you and me unconditionally. Like a good father or mother, God comes to us where we are, whatever our plight or predicament, and promises to be Emmanuel, God with us. God comes to us wherever we are, even in our darkness, and brings light and healing and hope. If we will look for God and listen for God, a new song can and will be born in us as it was in those who heard long ago.

The stories of scripture are recorded in order that we may know the truth, for the truth alone can set us free. We are guided and strengthened up by these stories. They bolster our faith throughout all of life.

As Luke tells us, Mary and Joseph had gone to Bethlehem for the Roman census and to pay their taxes. No room could be found in any guest quarters and Mary's baby was about to be born. Having been offered a stable with straw to lie in, Mary gave birth to her first son, wrapped him in bands of cloth, and laid him in a manger, a feed trough. Nothing could be remotely considered a home in that place. No comfortable reassurances of family or friends were to be found. No trusted persons were there to care for the exhausted mother, father, or their newborn infant. But God was there.

In the vulnerability of the baby Jesus, God entered the world in human flesh. In so doing, God came to be *with us* and God became *one of us*. For centuries God had been searching for ways to reach humanity and build a lasting covenant of love. God had tried the Law and various prophets, priests, and kings. However, people continued to go their own way, living lives filled with much activity but little sense of purpose. Although many believed in a God who could change history, few expected to encounter that God in a direct way. God, however, had a different plan.

The story of Jesus' birth is not to be seen as merely quaint or nostalgic, a picture postcard image of a better, bygone day. When we understand the significance of the birth of Jesus, we are energized and filled with hope, faith, and new perspective. The story of Almighty God becoming one of us helps us to *sing a song of our own* for the Savior.

How so, you may wonder? A couple of ways seem evident. First, we are *humbled*. We find the quality of humility to be universally present in all who have close encounters with God. Humility opens us to divine good news and instruction. Mary and Joseph listened to the words of God and humbly obeyed them.

Second, those who are faithful, who desire to sing a song for the Savior, are *teachable and open*. Mary and Joseph were surprised by the angel, as were the shepherds. In every case, they remained open to what the angel had to say to them. They did not close their hearts when they encountered God in a way that was initially frightening and unusual.

We often find in the scriptures that God breaks into humanity's well-ordered reverie and asks us to follow in faith, placing our trust in God. God steps in and wants to teach us or show us something more than we have experienced thus far. The nativity stories reassure us that when God is at work, even if it seems unusual, difficult, unfamiliar, or even unfair, *God will always work for our well being.* We can trust God to work on our behalf. We can count on God to love us. We are best off when we remain humble, teachable, and open to God's activity and God's surprises.

Our great God continues to break into human circumstances and pain to show us that he is alive and that he cares. God is not a distant, abstract deity to be feared. The Bible declares that God is love (1 John 4:8). God desires a close, personal relationship with you and me. God understands our hopes and dreams, our fears and insecurities. God knows all about our failures, but God also knows our fullest potential and every strength we possess. How is this possible? It is possible because God created us and gave us life.

Christians believe in a living, active, involved God. God does for us what we cannot do for ourselves. God became flesh, a human being. In Jesus Christ, God became like us in every way except sin (Hebrews 2:17-18; 4:15). Therefore, God fully understands our condition and our need.

God's Son longs to be your Savior from sin and the Leader of your life. He desires you and me to offer him the broken, confused, imperfect things in our lives. In exchange, he will give us faith, hope, and love. He will give us a new song! What an incredibly wonderful exchange! His wholeness is exchanged for our brokenness; his life for our sin and separation; his perfect love substituted for our imperfection. I hope that you will not hesitate to accept this profound gift-exchange. In so doing, it will likely be the best Christmas you have ever experienced.

Accepting Christ in this way is God's greatest gift to you and me. The gift was given long ago but remains fresh, alive, relevant, waiting for each of us to receive this evening. As the Bible says, "For God so loved the world that he gave his only Son, so that everyone who believes in him may not perish but may have eternal life" (John 3:16).

You and I were created for this. We were made by God for a deep, personal relationship of faith. When we accept this gift, we are transformed. A new significance and a remarkable joy take hold of us. Profound peace possesses us despite the sorrows, the painful circumstances, the confusion and frustrations of life. A new song is born in our hearts. When this happens, we know that God is with us; we are not alone. Thanks be to God!

Let us pray. Loving God, thank you for creating us and for caring so much about us that you sent your only Son, Jesus, to be with us. When we are afraid, calm us. When we are confused, clarify what you are trying to teach us. Wherever we have doubted you or mistrusted you, grant us clarity and reveal yourself to us. Reassure each one here of your care. Help us to know and to experience deep within the power of your love. Grant us the humility, the teachable spirit, and the openness to you that will give rise to a new song, a song of freedom, a song of joy, a song of hope and life everlasting. We pray these things in your glorious name, Lord Jesus. Amen.

Candle Lighting Ceremony
Please turn now in your bulletin and read the printed instructions listed under the "Candle Lighting Ceremony." For safety's sake, we especially want to highlight keeping your lighted candles upright and dipping the unlit candles toward the flame as you pass it down your row. In a few moments, we will begin this ceremony as the Worship Leader lights his candle from the Christ Candle in the center of the Advent Wreath. Light and love are two things which a person can give away without diminishing the source. Sharing our light and love increases these gifts rather than diminishing them. I hope that you will joyously share the light and love of God with your family, friends, and neighbors, not only this night, but in the new year.

When the appropriate lights are turned off, the choir will then sing, "Shine The Light Of Your Love" (or another anthem). During this anthem, those assisting with the lighting of the candles will come forward, receive the light from the Worship Leader and me and pass their light to those at the end of each pew. We will then join in the singing of "Silent Night" followed by praying the Lord's Prayer with our eyes open. We ask that you will remain seated and in reverent silence until the lights are turned on at the conclusion of the service. Let us now share in the Candle Lighting Ceremony.

www.ingramcontent.com/pod-product-compliance
Lightning Source LLC
Chambersburg PA
CBHW071756040426
42446CB00012B/2582